GOER MC PHASE 1

MISSIONAL COMMUNITY STUDY GUIDE

BASED ON THE BOOK

Spiritual Multiplication
in the Real World

AUSTIN STONE EDITION

This study guide is based on the book *Spiritual Multiplication in the Real World* by Bob McNabb.

spiritualmultiplication.org

Scripture quotations are from The Holy Bible, English Standard Version® (ESV®), copyright © 2001 by Crossway, a publishing ministry of Good News Publishers. Used by permission. All rights reserved. Italics found in Scripture quotations reflect the author's own emphasis.

Spiritual Multiplication in the Real World: Missional Community Study Guide: Austin Stone Edition

Copyright © 2013 Robert C. McNabb

Second Printing

All rights reserved. No part of this publication may be reproduced or transmitted in any form or by any means—electronic, mechanical, digital, photocopy, recording, or any other—except for brief

CONTENTS

WEEK ONE
Introduction Meeting
7

WEEK TWO
Chapter 1: Stars and Sand
Chapter 2: Maybe Someone Else
11

WEEK THREE
Chapter 3: Trouble in Multiplication Paradise
Chapter 4: Soil
23

WEEK FOUR
Chapter 5: Essential Elements
35

WEEK 5
Chapter 6: Gone Fishing
47

WEEK SIX
Chapter 7: Parenthood
59

WEEK SEVEN
Chapter 8: Learning to Fly
71

WEEK EIGHT
Chapter 9: The Lost Aspect of Disciple-Making
83

WEEK NINE
Chapter 10: You Can!
95

WEEK TEN
Chapter 11: From Vision to Reality
107

APPENDIX

WHO SHOULD USE THIS STUDY GUIDE?

- Groups of six to twelve believers who are established in their walk with the Lord (Young believers who still need establishing in the faith would benefit more from being in a group that uses *Foundations: Missional Community Guidebook*.)
- Disciples who are ready to enter into the adventure of team evangelism and disciple-making
- People who are able to fulfill the requirements of the Team Covenant (next page)

WHAT ARE SOME OF THE MAJOR LEARNING OBJECTIVES OF THIS STUDY?

Participants will gain the following:

- A conviction for disciple-making efforts to be done in the context of a disciple-making team and movement as well as knowledge of the essential elements of a movement
- An understanding of the evangelism process and a commitment to practice those steps together with fellow teammates as part of a team evangelistic effort
- An overview of the disciple-making process and an understanding of how to move disciples from new birth to maturity to reproduction

HOW IS THIS STUDY GUIDE DIFFERENT FROM OTHER DISCIPLESHIP MATERIALS?

Most discipleship materials focus on knowledge acquisition. Their primary focus is to learn. The hope is that after learning, you will start doing. This study guide is different. The focus is on doing and building habits. As you build these habits, you will learn, and you will keep learning long after you finish these materials. The habits that you will work together to establish are:

- Daily Time with God (self-feeding on his Word)
- Evangelism
- Prayer for the Lost
- Scripture Memory
- Obedience
- Teamwork

A MISSIONAL COMMUNITY IS A DISCIPLE-MAKING TEAM.

The term "Missional Community" has become very popular. Because of this, it is used to mean a wide variety of things. With this in mind, we have chosen to use the term "disciple-making team" frequently in these materials as a clarifying synonym for missional community.

HOW IS A DISCIPLE-MAKING TEAM DIFFERENT FROM A SMALL-GROUP?

The purpose of a disciple-making team is to glorify God by making disciples of all nations. Increasing our biblical knowledge is not the goal, but that will happen. The purpose is not to fellowship and pray, although we will do those things. Finally, the purpose is not to hold us accountable to spiritual disciplines, though that will occur when we meet. As you can see, a disciple-making team differs from a small group, a discipleship group, a Bible study, or a prayer group. Of course, there is nothing wrong with being a part of any of those types of groups.

Disciple-making teams are different in that they seek to stay focused on fulfilling the Great Commission through the multiplication of disciple-makers and new disciple-making teams. This focus drives members into deeper times of fellowship, prayer, Bible study, and accountability as the team lives and ministers together in a missional community. Mission is not one of the purposes of the team; it is the reason the team exists.

═ TEAM COVENANT ═

By God's grace, I covenant with the other members of my team to:

- Spend at least three hours with Jesus each week.
- Spend at least two hours reaching out to the lost each week.
- Spend at least one hour in prayer for my lost friends and the world with others of this team each week.
- Arrive prepared and ready to contribute to the group each weekly Half-Time meeting.
- Begin discipling others within a few months of completing this study.

I will strive, by the grace of God, to meet the above commitments.

HOW CAN THIS GROUP DEVELOP LEADERS?

First, find an apprentice or co-leader who will help you lead the group. Hopefully, doing this with you will help prepare them to lead their own group soon.

Ideally, there will be at least two or three people out of the six to twelve in the group whom you can challenge to join as your apprentices.

The best people to consider for this are ones who:
- Have been established in their faith
- Have displayed faithfulness in passing on what they are taught
- Are teachable to you
- Have the availability to help you lead the group

Your strategy should be to spend extra time with these apprentices (like Jesus did with Peter, James, and John) and equip them to help lead the others in the community. This gets you discipling people in the context of ministry.

HOW TO CHALLENGE SOMEONE INTO THIS GROUP

PRAY AND ASK GOD TO BRING TO MIND THE NAMES OF SIX TO TWELVE PEOPLE WHO:

- Are already established in their faith
- Seem eager to evangelize and make disciples

SCHEDULE AN APPOINTMENT WITH THOSE YOU WILL CHALLENGE ONTO THE TEAM.

- Use the Sharing the Vision tool (p. 125)
- Go over the Purpose page and Team Covenant
- Take along one of your apprentices if possible

SET A DATE BY WHICH THEY MUST DECIDE.

WEEKLY 3-2-1

3 HOURS with Jesus

Everything begins with God. The foundation of a healthy personal ministry must be our own relationship with Christ. Therefore, commit to communing with him through prayer, worship, and reading his Word at least three hours a week.

2 HOURS with the lost

In order to reap, we must sow the seed of the gospel. We will spend at least two hours a week finding lost people, generating interest in Jesus, sharing the gospel, and Lord willing, helping them decide to follow Christ. Jesus sent his disciples two-by-two. In the same way, we want to go out two-by-two with other people on our team. We may not share the gospel every time, but we will always do something evangelistic, like meeting new people, sharing our testimonies, praying for people's needs, or inviting them to experience our community.

1 HOUR with each other in prayer

Jesus informs us that the key to the harvest is prayer. To see people enter into the Kingdom of God, we must become a people dedicated to prayer both privately and corporately. As a community, we will dedicate at least one hour of corporate prayer for the lost and the nations each week.

WEEKLY HALF-TIME MEETINGS

When it comes to spiritual multiplication, what happens all week long is more important than what happens in a once-a-week meeting. That's why we call our meetings "Half-Time." They're simply an opportunity to pause once a week and report on what God has been doing in the last six days, pray and encourage one another, plan our next week of ministry, and discuss the week's reading assignments. The components of each meeting are explained below.

WELCOME || 15 minutes

The Welcome portion will provide an opportunity to learn about the others in our community. Each week, we will have a different icebreaker question to discuss.

WITNESS || 10 minutes

The Witness time is an opportunity to share about what God did the previous week in our personal lives or in the lives of our family and friends. (Testimonies of what happened with our lost friends will occur during the Works section.) Be sure to write down a few notes in your workbook so you can look back and remember what God has done.

WORSHIP || 10 minutes

The Worship time is for our group to pray, sing, talk, or praise God in any other way that seems fitting to worship him for who he is and what he has done.

WORKS || 25 minutes

The Works time is for our group to share about what God is doing among our lost friends and plan for the next week's ministry.

Each week, we will write names of our lost friends on a large piece of light blue poster board or fabric called "Big Blue." (You can read "The Legend of Big Blue" on p. 122.) Names should only be added once you have a person's phone number and are likely to see them again. We will underline names of friends we are studying the Bible with and put a cross next to any people who start following Christ.

We will also start adding some of these names to our FISHing charts (p. 118) as we begin to share with them.

We will share how our ministry went in the past week and talk about any plans we need to make for the upcoming week.

WORLD || 10 minutes

The World time will help us learn a little more about the world in which we live. Each week, the "Know God's World" section will provide a few facts about the world. In the "Share Helpful Resources" section, a different team member will take responsibility for learning about the resource of the week and then share about it with the team. We will choose one person to research and share for the next week. We will finish the World time in prayer for the nations.

WORD || 20 minutes

The Word time gives our community an opportunity to discuss the "Daily Quiet Times" and the "Learning Questions" from *Spiritual Multiplication in the Real World* from the previous week. This time will also be used to review the "Key Verse."

GAME PLAN

This is a convenient list of everything we need to do before next week's Half-Time. We will use this to keep track of assignments and set goals.

LEARNING QUESTIONS

Each week, we will be assigned one or two chapters from the book *Spiritual Multiplication in the Real World*. There are questions in this workbook that will help guide our learning and discussion. We will complete our reading and answer the questions before we show up to Half-Time each week.

DAILY QUIET TIMES

Each week, we will have a set of Daily Quiet Times to guide our three hours of time with God. These readings go along with the topics of *Spiritual Multiplication in the Real World*. Each of us should read the verses in context to get the full picture of what is being said.

KEY VERSE

These are important verses that come from our weekly readings. Each week, we will memorize the assigned verse and be prepared to recite it at the Half-Time meeting.

WEEK ONE
Introduction Meeting

Called to a people not a place
What was mission like

WELCOME || 15 MINUTES

Have everyone introduce themselves by answering these questions:
- What is your name?
- Why do you want to be in a disciple-making team?

Take some time to familiarize yourselves with this entire workbook.

Read through together and discuss the Introduction (p. 1-6).

Sign the Covenant (p. 2).

WITNESS || 10 MINUTES

What did you see God do this week?

WORSHIP || 10 MINUTES

Thank God together in prayer for what he did last week.

Use an iPod, guitar, etc. and sing a few songs together.

WORKS || 25 MINUTES

FISHING CHART

Turn to the FISHing chart (p. 118). Take a few minutes to write down the names of your lost friends and relatives who live in the same town as you. If you don't have ten, then make a plan to meet new people this week.

BIG BLUE

As a group, write the names of your lost friends on the large piece of poster board or fabric we are calling "Big Blue." After all the names are written, circle around and pray for your friends.

TOOLS

The leader should introduce "My Story: Interest-Creating Testimony" (p. 120) and then demonstrate how to share it by telling their own using the outline. You will be working on your story throughout this week and will practice sharing it at Half-Time next week.

ACTIVITY

Turn to the Game Plan on the next page and fill in your goals for this week.

GAME PLAN FOR NEXT WEEK

3 HOURS *with Jesus*

Daily Quiet Times
Memorize Key Verse: Mark 4:20

2 HOURS *with lost people*

If your FISHing chart is not full, meet new people
I will meet _____ new people this week

1 HOUR *with each other in prayer*

This week I will pray with _____

LEARNING ASSIGNMENT

Complete "My Story: Creating Interest Testimony" worksheet (p. 120)
Read *Spiritual Multiplication in the Real World* (Ch. 1-2) and answer the Learning Questions

WEEK TWO

Chapter 1: Stars and Sand
Chapter 2: Maybe Someone Else

KEY VERSE

Mark 4:20
But those that were sown on the good soil are the ones who hear the word and accept it and bear fruit, thirtyfold and sixtyfold and a hundredfold.

ORD

Observations about God's intentions for mankind	Observations about God's character

Genesis 1:27-28

| We were intended to have his attributes. Even the attribute of authority + dominion. | God extended a level of trust to let us rule on earth + oversee it. He wants us. |

Genesis 9:1-2

| He wanted Noah + sons to fill the earth. The animals would fear them thus submission + would not impede their expansion | He wants us to be successful in filling the earth. + equips us for that. |

Revelation 7:9-12

| Every people will praise god. It's in our hearts to love god. | Only he can forgive sin/offer salvation. He is the source + apex of glory, wisdom, honor, power + might |

WORSHIP

Praise God for what you saw about him in the Word today.
How those established in their relationship + work for god can cultivate, direct, + strengthen those that aren't yet as established in the relationship/work for god.

Today I thank God for...
Finding a brother that could lend me a hand.

I will worship God by obeying in the following ways this week:
Offer regular praise. Rev. 7:12

Today I will trust God for...
~~My car~~ My purpose in work, not career. ~~but~~ work lifelong.

God's attributes

Melchizedek

WORD

Observations about God's promises	Observations about God's character
Genesis 22:9-18 Through great faith we've inherited a great blessing. vs18 "And in your offspring shall all the nations of the earth be blessed"	God requires limitless faith. For limitless faith Abraham was + multiplied. Faith with actions
Hebrews 6:13-20 God's promises are not suggestion but direct + factual	God is the guarantor of his promises because of benevolence/authority.
Galatians 3:7-9 Those who are in faith are blessed along with Abraham. If it was ever promised by god, he will make it happen.	God stands by his word that Abraham's blessing would be shared with all nations. God still requires faith.

How do the promises made to Abraham apply to you?
Through Abraham + the promise god made for the nations, my forefathers + myself are known by god.

Describe the encouragement you find in these verses.
God wants my faith + it pleases him. He stands by his word.

Write a specific life goal related to multiplication that you would like to trust God to accomplish through your life.
To humbly + nobly ~~serve his people~~ share the hope we god gives.

WORSHIP

Praise God for what you saw about him in the Word today.
1st Peter even as we suffer we ~~trust~~ know that it's not in vein.

Today I thank God for...
The reverence I feel for him

I will worship God by obeying in the following ways this week:
Offer regular praise.

WORD

Principles of spiritual multiplication observed	Observations about God's character

2 Timothy 1

WORSHIP

Praise God for what you saw about him in the Word today.

Today I thank God for...

I will worship God by obeying in the following ways this week:

Today I will trust God for...

WORD

Principles of spiritual multiplication observed	Observations about God's character

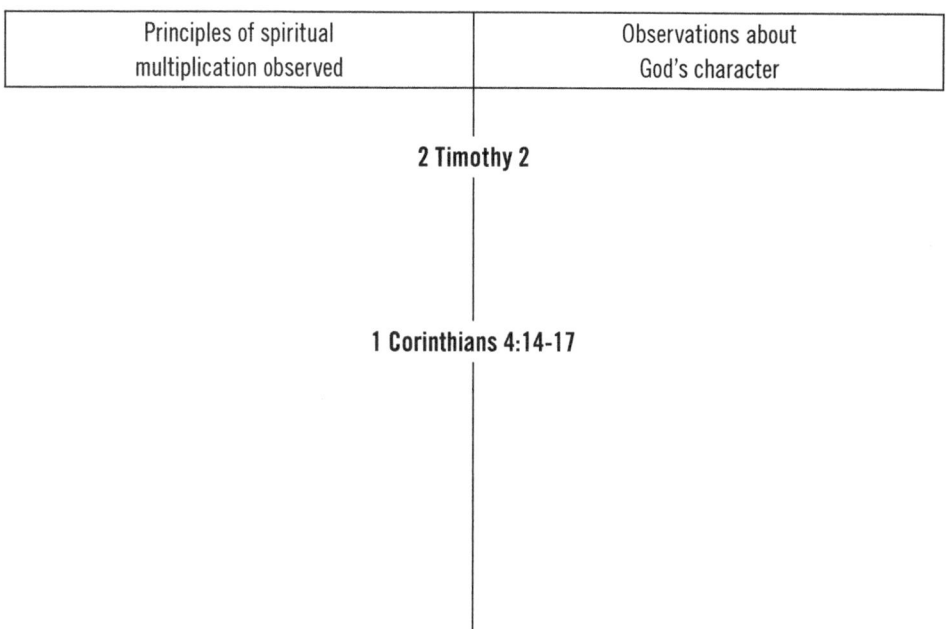

2 Timothy 2

1 Corinthians 4:14-17

WORSHIP

Praise God for what you saw about him in the Word today.

Today I thank God for...

I will worship God by obeying in the following ways this week:

Today I will trust God for...

WORD

Principles of spiritual multiplication observed	Observations about God's character
2 Timothy 3 (especially verses 10-11)	

WORSHIP

Praise God for what you saw about him in the Word today.

Today I thank God for...

I will worship God by obeying in the following ways this week:

Today I will trust God for...

WORD

Principles of spiritual multiplication observed	Observations about God's character

2 Timothy 4

WORSHIP

Praise God for what you saw about him in the Word today.

Today I thank God for...

I will worship God by obeying in the following ways this week:

Today I will trust God for...

SUMMARY AND REFLECTION DAY

After looking over this week's quiet times, summarize what God has been teaching you.

What specific action will you take to apply what you have learned?

Did you really meet with Jesus this week, or did you just go through the motions?

WORSHIP

Praise God for what you saw about him in the Word this week.

Today I thank God for...

I will worship God by obeying in the following ways this week:

Today I will trust God for...

▷ Write out this week's Key Verse below:

SPIRITUAL MULTIPLICATION IN THE REAL WORLD (Chapters 1-2)

1. How did you answer the four questions from page 1:

    - Is it hard for you to believe God wants to multiply your life and make your spiritual descendants as numerous as the stars in the sky and the sand on the seashore? Why or why not?

    - What are you specifically asking God to do through your life?

    - How many men or women are you asking God to equip as multiplying disciples through you?

    - How many nations are you asking God to impact through you? Describe how reading about the doctrine of multiplication impacted you.

2. Spiritual multiplication is God's plan for reaching the world, and he has no Plan B. In light of this, how should we respond to failure in our efforts to multiply?

3. What lies do you think Satan wants Christians to believe about spiritual multiplication in the real world? What lies have you believed?

4. In light of God's awesome power, is there something big you want to trust God to do through your life this year?

5. What is your number one takeaway from reading Chapters 1-2?

WELCOME || 15 MINUTES

Have each person answer the question:

> Who has had the greatest impact on your spiritual life?

Split into pairs and share your Interest-Creating Testimony with a partner, giving each other feedback on how to make your story more clear or interest-creating.

WITNESS || 10 MINUTES

What did you see God do this week?

WORSHIP || 10 MINUTES

Thank God together in prayer for what he did last week.

Use an iPod, guitar, etc. and sing a few songs together.

WORKS || 25 MINUTES

FISHING CHART

Turn to the FISHing chart (p. 118) and write names of your lost friends on it.

The ideal people to have on your FISHing Chart are people:

> Whom you will be able to see repeatedly
>
> Who would be open to your influence

Discuss as a team where and how each of you can meet people who fulfill the two criteria above.

> It's okay if you can't fill the chart this week. You will be working as a team to fill in new people in the coming weeks.

Turn to p. 121 and read about asking questions, then decide how many people

BIG BLUE

Get out your Big Blue and write in the names of the new lost friends you met this week. When all the names have been written, put the list in the middle of the group and pray for those listed. Do not hurry this prayer time. It is the life blood of your ministry as a team and should therefore be central in each of your meetings.

ACTIVITY

Turn to the Game Plan on the next page and fill in your goals for this week.

WORLD || 10 MINUTES

KNOW GOD'S WORLD: Missionaries

Ninety-nine percent of believers live and work among the 60 percent of the world's population that already has the gospel.

Only 10 percent of missionaries work among the 40 percent of the world's population that is considered unreached.

Three out of every five non-Christians live beyond the reach of same-culture evangelism. Someone will have to intentionally cross cultural or language barriers to reach them.[1]

SHARE HELPFUL RESOURCES

Assign next week's resource:
Global Prayer Digest (globalprayerdigest.org)

PRAY FOR THE NATIONS

Share Mark 4:20 with a partner.

Discuss the major learning points and application steps from your Daily Quiet Times (Day 7).

Discuss your answers to the Learning Questions for *Spiritual Multiplication in the Real World* (Ch. 1-2).

Close with prayer.

GAME PLAN FOR NEXT WEEK

3 HOURS *with Jesus*

Daily Quiet Times
Memorize Key Verse: Acts 2:46-47

2 HOURS *with lost people*

If your FISHing chart is not full, meet new people.
I will meet _____ new people this week

Share your story
I will share my story with _____ people this week

My ministry partner this week will be _____

1 HOUR *with each other in prayer*

This week I will pray with _____

LEARNING ASSIGNMENT

WEEK THREE

Chapter 3: Trouble in Multiplication Paradise
Chapter 4: Soil

KEY VERSE

Acts 2:46-47
And day by day, attending the temple together and breaking bread in their homes, they received their food with glad and generous hearts, praising God and having favor with all the people. And the Lord added to their number day by day those who were being saved.

RD

Foundations for ministry that were laid	Observations about God's will and his ways

Acts 1

WORSHIP

Praise God for what you saw about him in the Word today.

Today I thank God for...

I will worship God by obeying in the following ways this week:

Today I will trust God for...

WORD

Observations about living in community and disciple-making as a team	Ways in which God displayed his goodness

Acts 2

WORSHIP

Praise God for what you saw about him in the Word today.

Today I thank God for...

I will worship God by obeying in the following ways this week:

Today I will trust God for...

WORD

Observations about living in community and disciple-making as a team	Ways in which God displayed his goodness
Acts 3	

WORSHIP

Praise God for what you saw about him in the Word today.

Today I thank God for...

I will worship God by obeying in the following ways this week:

Today I will trust God for...

WORD

Observations about living in community and teamwork	Observations about Jesus

Acts 4

WORSHIP

Praise God for what you saw about him in the Word today.

Today I thank God for...

I will worship God by obeying in the following ways this week:

Today I will trust God for...

WORD

Observations about the importance of unity	Observations about the attributes of God
Acts 5	
John 17:20-23	
Romans 15:5-9	

WORSHIP

Praise God for what you saw about him in the Word today.

Today I thank God for...

I will worship God by obeying in the following ways this week:

Today I will trust God for...

WORD

Benefits of teamwork	Observations about God's grace in suffering

Acts 6

WORSHIP

Praise God for what you saw about him in the Word today.

Today I thank God for...

I will worship God by obeying in the following ways this week:

Today I will trust God for...

SUMMARY AND REFLECTION DAY

After looking over this week's quiet times, summarize what God has been teaching you.

What specific action will you take to apply what you have learned?

Did you really meet with Jesus this week, or did you just go through the motions?

WORSHIP

Praise God for what you saw about him in the Word this week.

Today I thank God for...

I will worship God by obeying in the following ways this week:

Today I will trust God for...

▷ Write out this week's Key Verse below:

SPIRITUAL MULTIPLICATION IN THE REAL WORLD (Chapters 3-4)

1. Have you ever tried to multiply spiritually? If so, how did it go?

2. Respond to the statement, "If you're not fishing, you're not following." Why do you agree or disagree?

3. Describe the type of group that you will need to be a part of if you are going to multiply your life consistently over the coming years.

4. What thoughts come to mind when you read about the impact your life could have if you too applied the biblical principles practiced by highly effective disciple-makers?

5. How do you think American individualism has affected the way we think about disciple-making?

6. What specific action step do you need to take to apply what you learned in your reading this week?

WELCOME || 15 MINUTES

Have each person answer the question:

> What is one book (besides the Bible) that has impacted your spiritual life?

Split into pairs and share your story with a new partner, giving each other feedback on how to make your story more clear or interest-creating.

WITNESS || 10 MINUTES

What did you see God do this week?

WORSHIP || 10 MINUTES

Thank God together in prayer for what he did last week.

Make a list of the names of God and praise him for his attributes.

WORKS || 25 MINUTES

FISHING CHART
Update your FISHing chart with any new people you met this week or steps you took in the FISHing process.

BIG BLUE
Add your team's new friends to Big Blue. Put the list in the middle of the group and pray over your friends.

ACTIVITY
Turn to p. 122 and read about a Matthew Party. Then spend some time as a group planning one together.

Turn to the Game Plan on the next page and fill in your goals for this week.

WORLD || 10 MINUTES

KNOW GOD'S WORLD: Money

Of foreign mission funding, 87 percent is used for work among those already Christian. Twelve percent of funding is spent for work among those who are already evangelized but non-Christians. One percent is used for work among unevangelized and unreached people.[1] According to the National Retail Federation, in 2011, Americans spent the same amount on Halloween costumes (for their pets!).

Do you know of ways that you can ensure that a more significant portion of your giving goes to reaching those who have never heard of Jesus?

SHARE HELPFUL RESOURCES
Report on this week's resource: Global Prayer Digest (globalprayerdigest.org)

Assign next week's resource: Finishing the Task (finishingthetask.com)

PRAY FOR THE NATIONS

WORD || 20 MINUTES

Share Acts 2:46-47 with a partner.

Discuss the major learning points and application steps from your Daily Quiet Times (Day 7).

Discuss your answers to the Learning Questions for *Spiritual Multiplication in the Real World* (Ch. 3-4).

Close with prayer.

GAME PLAN FOR NEXT WEEK

3 HOURS *with Jesus*

Daily Quiet Times
Memorize Key Verse: Hebrews 10:24-25

2 HOURS *with lost people*

If your FISHing chart is not full, meet new people and use the Interest-Creating Questions.
I will meet _____ new people this week

Share your story
I will share my story with _____ people this week

My ministry partner this week will be _____

Plan a Matthew Party

1 HOUR *with each other in prayer*

This week I will pray with _____

LEARNING ASSIGNMENT

WEEK FOUR

Chapter 5: Essential Elements

KEY VERSE

Hebrews 10:24-25
And let us consider how to stir up one another to love and good works, not neglecting to meet together, as is the habit of some, but encouraging one another, and all the more as you see the Day drawing near.

WORD

Observations about vision and vision casting	Observations about the kingdom
	Matthew 4:19 It has many different people with different skills chosen
	Matthew 6:19-21 Don't be distracted by pleasures of earth. Let your treasure be Loving your Father + serving him in your life
	Matthew 13:1-52 We are chosen. The Kingdom is hidden but valuable beyond measure.

What do you need to do to put yourself in a situation where you are consistently challenged with an eternal and multiplying vision?

Whom do you need to encourage this week, and how will you cast vision with them?

WORSHIP

Praise God for what you saw about him in the Word today.

Today I thank God for...

I will worship God by obeying in the following ways this week:

Today I will trust God for...

WORD

What do you observe regarding the role of modeling in spiritual multiplication?

    John 13:15

    2 Thessalonians 3:9

    Titus 2:7-8

    1 Corinthians 4:16-17

    1 Corinthians 11:1

What attribute of Christ do you most admire and want to model for those you disciple?

WORSHIP

Praise God for what you saw about him in the Word today.

Leading us to Freedom

Today I thank God for...

I will worship God by obeying in the following ways this week:

Today I will trust God for...

WORD

Observations regarding training and coaching	Observations about Jesus

Matthew 17

WORSHIP

Praise God for what you saw about him in the Word today.

Today I thank God for...

I will worship God by obeying in the following ways this week:

Today I will trust God for...

WORD

Examples of Jesus' ministry to the masses	Examples of Jesus' ministry to the few
Matthew 5:1-2	
Matthew 7:28-29	
Mark 3:13-15	
Mark 9:30-31	

Why is ministry to both the masses and the few important?

What relationship do you see between ministry to the masses and ministry to the few in spiritual multiplication?

Do you think you need to increase your ministry to the masses or the few? What steps will you take?

How do you see Jesus' love in his ministry to the masses and the few?

WORSHIP

Praise God for what you saw about him in the Word today.

Today I thank God for...

I will worship God by obeying in the following ways this week:

WORD

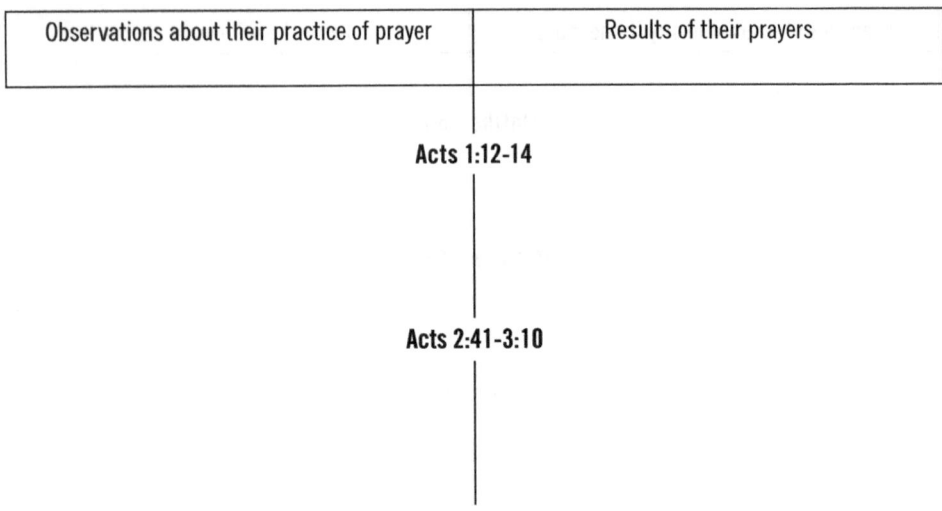

What steps will you take to devote yourself to prayer?

WORSHIP

Praise God for what you saw about him in the Word today.

Today I thank God for...

I will worship God by obeying in the following ways this week:

Today I will trust God for...

WORD

Purpose for retreat (Each passage gives a different reason)	Observations about Jesus

Mark 6:30-32

Luke 9:28-36

Mark 9:30-31

Do you need to plan a retreat soon? For what purpose?

WORSHIP

Praise God for what you saw about him in the Word today.

Today I thank God for...

I will worship God by obeying in the following ways this week:

Today I will trust God for...

SUMMARY AND REFLECTION DAY

After looking over this week's quiet times, summarize what God has been teaching you.

What specific action will you take to apply what you have learned?

Did you really meet with Jesus this week, or did you just go through the motions?

WORSHIP

Praise God for what you saw about him in the Word this week.

Today I thank God for...

I will worship God by obeying in the following ways this week:

Today I will trust God for...

▷ Write out this week's Key Verse below:

SPIRITUAL MULTIPLICATION IN THE REAL WORLD (Chapter 5)

1. What are the differences between a church that is designed to grow in attendance and one that is designed to equip and help its members multiply their lives?

2. Why is it so important to be part of a church that possesses the seven essential elements of a disciple-making movement?

3. What do you think the author is saying are the main differences between a standard small group and a disciple-making team?

4. What is your major takeaway from this chapter? How will you apply what you learned?

WELCOME || 15 MINUTES

Have each person answer the question:

> Who do you know that most models the vision of spiritual multiplication? Why did you pick this person?

Split into pairs and share your story with a new partner, giving each other feedback on how to make your story more clear or interest-creating.

WITNESS || 10 MINUTES

What did you see God do this week?

WORSHIP || 10 MINUTES

Thank God together in prayer for what he did last week.

Read Psalm 136 responsively: one person reads the first half of a verse, and everyone reads the second half together.

WORKS || 25 MINUTES

FISHING CHART
Update your FISHing chart with any new people you met this week or steps you took in the FISHing process.

BIG BLUE
Add your team's new friends to Big Blue. Put the list in the middle of the group and pray over your friends.

ACTIVITY
Turn to the Game Plan on the next page and fill in your goals for this week.

WORLD || 10 MINUTES

KNOW GOD'S WORLD: 10/40 Window

Eighty-six percent of all unreached people groups lie within the region called the 10/40 window, which is between 10 and 40 degrees north latitude, from the west coast of Africa to the east coast of Asia.[2]

These people are not "more lost" than your unsaved neighbor or family member, but they are "unreached" in the sense that they have not had the opportunity to hear the Gospel.[4]

SHARE HELPFUL RESOURCES
Report on this week's resource: Finishing the Task (finishingthetask.com)

Assign next week's resource: Open Doors (opendoors.org)

PRAY FOR THE NATIONS

WORD || 20 MINUTES

Share Hebrews 10:24-25 with a partner.

Discuss the major learning points and application steps from your Daily Quiet Times (Day 7).

Discuss your answers to the Learning Questions for *Spiritual Multiplication in the Real World* (Ch. 5).

Close with prayer.

GAME PLAN FOR NEXT WEEK

3 HOURS *with Jesus*

Daily Quiet Times
Memorize Key Verse: John 13:35

2 HOURS *with lost people*

If your FISHing chart is not full, meet new people and use the Interest-Creating Questions.
I will meet _____ new people this week

Share your story
I will share my story with _____ people this week

My ministry partner this week will be _____

1 HOUR *with each other in prayer*

This week I will pray with _____

LEARNING ASSIGNMENT

1. Poo Time
   ≤ Subtle its hard for me to meet some people where they are @

   Self starting/sticking to the work
   FD in
   adop christ

① role/responsibility self
② vision for personal growth
③ Disciples who / do you want
④

WEEK FIVE

Chapter 6: Gone Fishing

KEY VERSE

John 13:35
By this all people will know that you are my disciples, if you have love for one another.

WORD

Observations about evangelism	How Jesus created interest

John 4:1-45

What do you observe about Jesus in this passage that impresses you?

WORSHIP

Praise God for what you saw about him in the Word today.

Today I thank God for...

I will worship God by obeying in the following ways this week:

Today I will trust God for...

WORD

In Luke 10:1, how did Jesus send his disciples out to do evangelism?

What advantages do you see in approaching evangelism as a team rather than as individuals?

    John 13:34-35

    1 Corinthians 14:24-25

In light of these verses, what changes will you make to how you evangelize?

WORSHIP

Praise God for what you saw about him in the Word today.

Today I thank God for...

I will worship God by obeying in the following ways this week:

Today I will trust God for...

WORD

Observations about evangelism	Observations about God

Acts 17:16-31

Finding out about people

Interesting people in the gospel

Sharing the good news

Helping people make a decision

In light of these verses, what changes will you make to how you evangelize?

WORSHIP

Praise God for what you saw about him in the Word today.

Today I thank God for…

I will worship God by obeying in the following ways this week:

Today I will trust God for…

WORD

Observations about evangelism	Observations about God

1 Corinthians 3:1-23

WORSHIP

Praise God for what you saw about him in the Word today.

Today I thank God for...

I will worship God by obeying in the following ways this week:

Today I will trust God for...

WORD

Observations about evangelism	Observations about Jesus

Matthew 11:25-30

Observations about creating interest

Observations about calling people to a decision

WORSHIP

Praise God for what you saw about him in the Word today.

Today I thank God for...

I will worship God by obeying in the following ways this week:

Today I will trust God for...

WORD

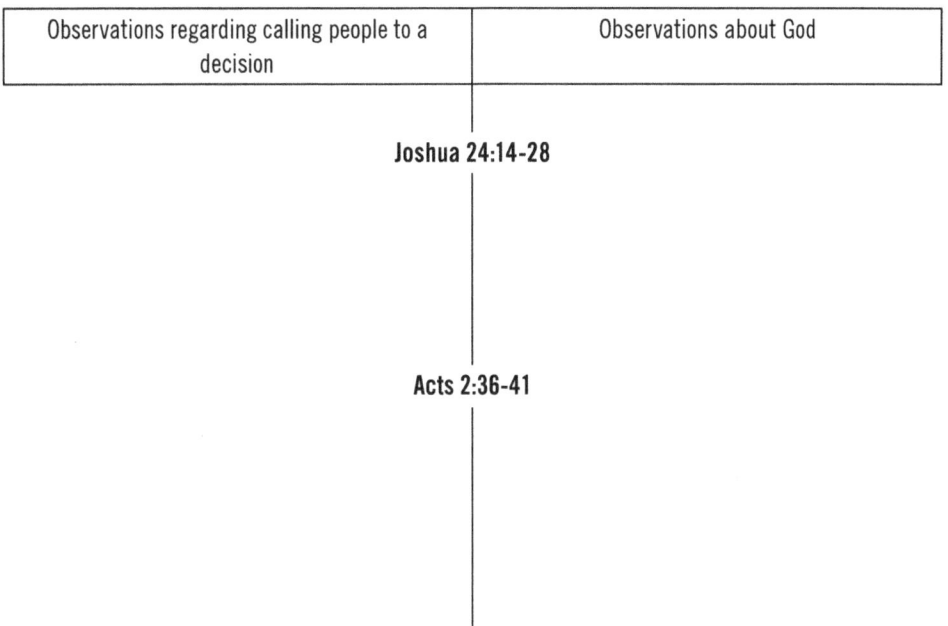

Observations regarding calling people to a decision	Observations about God

Joshua 24:14-28

Acts 2:36-41

Is there someone you need to invite to follow Jesus this week?

WORSHIP

Praise God for what you saw about him in the Word today.

Today I thank God for...

I will worship God by obeying in the following ways this week:

Today I will trust God for...

SUMMARY AND REFLECTION DAY

After looking over this week's quiet times, summarize what God has been teaching you.

What specific action will you take to apply what you have learned?

Did you really meet with Jesus this week, or did you just go through the motions?

WORSHIP

Praise God for what you saw about him in the Word this week.

Today I thank God for...

I will worship God by obeying in the following ways this week:

Today I will trust God for...

▷ Write out this week's Key Verse below:

SPIRITUAL MULTIPLICATION IN THE REAL WORLD (Chapter 6)

1. What was something new you learned from your reading this week?

2. Evaluate yourself in the following areas and share your answers with the group.
   (1 = Weakness, 3 = Average, 5 = Strength)

   ____ Finding new people with whom to share the gospel

   ____ Finding out about people's lives (asking good questions)

   ____ Creating interest

   ____ Sharing the Gospel

   ____ Helping people make a decision and deal with barriers

3. What steps will you take to grow in your weak areas?

WELCOME || 15 MINUTES

Have each person answer the question:

> What is the best news you have ever heard (besides the gospel)?
>
> How long did it take you to start telling others about your good news?

Split into pairs and share your story with a new partner, giving each other feedback on how to make your story more clear or interest-creating.

WITNESS || 10 MINUTES

What did you see God do this week?

WORSHIP || 10 MINUTES

Thank God together in prayer for what he did last week.

Have a time of silence before the Lord to hear his voice and worship. Ask him to bring to mind a verse you could use to worship him or encourage the group. Pray the verse back to the Lord.

WORKS || 25 MINUTES

FISHING CHART
Update your FISHing chart with any new people you met this week or steps you took in the FISHing process.

BIG BLUE
Add your team's new friends to Big Blue. Put the list in the middle of the group and pray over your friends.

ACTIVITY
Turn to the Game Plan on the next page and fill in your goals for this week.

WORLD || 10 MINUTES

KNOW GOD'S WORLD: Tribals

There are 161 million people in 704 tribal people groups.[1]

They have animistic and superstitious beliefs (everything has a spirit, such as water, rocks, trees, animals).

They must be careful not to offend these spirits and must appease them with sacrifices.

They often worship idols and ancestors and visit witch doctors.

SHARE HELPFUL RESOURCES
Report on this week's resource:
Open Doors (opendoors.org)

Assign next week's resource:
Voice of the Martyrs (persecution.org)

PRAY FOR THE NATIONS

WORD || 20 MINUTES

Share John 13:35 with a partner.

Discuss the major learning points and application steps from your Daily Quiet Times (Day 7).

Discuss your answers to the Learning Questions for *Spiritual Multiplication in the Real World* (Ch. 6).

GAME PLAN FOR NEXT WEEK

3 HOURS *with Jesus*

Daily Quiet Times
Memorize Key Verse: 1 Thessalonians 2:7-8

2 HOURS *with lost people*

I will create interest with _____ (person on FISHing chart) by doing _____ (interest-creating activity).

My ministry partner this week will be _____

1 HOUR *with each other in prayer*

This week I will pray with _____

LEARNING ASSIGNMENT

Read *Spiritual Multiplication in the Real World* (Ch. 7) and answer the Learning Questions

WEEK SIX

Chapter 7: Parenthood

KEY VERSE

1 Thessalonians 2:7-8
But we were gentle among you, like a nursing mother taking care of her own children. So, being affectionately desirous of you, we were ready to share with you not only the gospel of God but also our own selves, because you had become very dear to us.

WORD

Observations about discipling relationships	Observations about God

1 Thessalonians 1

WORSHIP

Praise God for what you saw about him in the Word today.

Today I thank God for...

I will worship God by obeying in the following ways this week:

Today I will trust God for...

WORD

Observations about discipling relationships	Observations about God

1 Thessalonians 2

WORSHIP

Praise God for what you saw about him in the Word today.

Today I thank God for...

I will worship God by obeying in the following ways this week:

Today I will trust God for...

WORD

Observations about discipling relationships	Observations about God

1 Thessalonians 3

WORSHIP

Praise God for what you saw about him in the Word today.

Today I thank God for...

I will worship God by obeying in the following ways this week:

Today I will trust God for...

WORD

Observations about discipling relationships	Observations about God

1 Thessalonians 4

WORSHIP

Praise God for what you saw about him in the Word today.

Today I thank God for...

I will worship God by obeying in the following ways this week:

Today I will trust God for...

WORD

Observations about discipling relationships	Observations about God

1 Thessalonians 5

WORSHIP

Praise God for what you saw about him in the Word today.

Today I thank God for...

I will worship God by obeying in the following ways this week:

Today I will trust God for...

WORD

Foundations of faith mentioned	Observations about God

Hebrews 6:1-2

Ephesians 1:15-23

Ephesians 3:14-19

WORSHIP

Praise God for what you saw about him in the Word today.

Today I thank God for...

I will worship God by obeying in the following ways this week:

Today I will trust God for...

SUMMARY AND REFLECTION DAY

After looking over this week's quiet times, summarize what God has been teaching you.

What specific action will you take to apply what you have learned?

Did you really meet with Jesus this week, or did you just go through the motions?

WORSHIP

Praise God for what you saw about him in the Word this week.

Today I thank God for...

I will worship God by obeying in the following ways this week:

Today I will trust God for...

▷ Write out this week's Key Verse below:

SPIRITUAL MULTIPLICATION IN THE REAL WORLD (Chapter 7)

1. What are the needs of a new disciple?

2. What are some of the key things a disciple-maker can do to help a new believer become established in the faith?

3. What are some traps to avoid when establishing new believers?

4. Why does the author discourage discipling someone one-on-one?

5. What specific application steps do you believe you need to take in light of what you read in this chapter?

6. With whom will you share what you learned in this chapter?

WELCOME || 15 MINUTES

Share a story of an answered prayer.

WITNESS || 10 MINUTES

What did you see God do this week?

WORSHIP || 10 MINUTES

Thank God together in prayer for what he did last week.

Use an iPod, guitar, etc. and sing a few songs together.

WORKS || 25 MINUTES

FISHING CHART
Update your FISHing chart with any new people you met this week or steps you took in the FISHing process.

BIG BLUE
Add your team's new friends to Big Blue. Put the list in the middle of the group and pray over your friends.

TOOLS
The leader should introduce "The Bridge Illustration" (p. 123) and then demonstrate how to share it.

Pair up and practice The Bridge with another teammate, giving each other feedback.

ACTIVITY
Plan another Matthew Party as a group.

Turn to the Game Plan on the next page

WORLD || 10 MINUTES

KNOW GOD'S WORLD: Hindus

There are 860 million people in 1,843 Hindu people groups.[1]

They believe in millions of gods.

They worship idols of clay, stone, or pictures by giving them food, flowers, and money.

They believe they are caught in a cycle of birth-death-rebirth called reincarnation.

SHARE HELPFUL RESOURCES
Report on this week's resource: Voice of the Martyrs (persecution.org)

Assign next week's resource: Perspectives on the World Christian Movement (perspectives.org)

PRAY FOR THE NATIONS

WORD || 20 MINUTES

Share 1 Thessalonians 2:7-8 with a partner.

Discuss the major learning points and application steps from your Daily Quiet Times (Day 7).

Discuss your answers to the Learning Questions for *Spiritual Multiplication in the Real World* (Ch. 7).

Close with prayer.

GAME PLAN FOR NEXT WEEK

3 HOURS *with Jesus*

Daily Quiet Times
Memorize Key Verse: Ephesians 4:11-12

2 HOURS *with lost people*

Plan a Matthew Party

Share The Bridge
I will share The Bridge with _____ people this week

My ministry partner this week will be _____

1 HOUR *with each other in prayer*

This week I will pray with _____

LEARNING ASSIGNMENT

Read *Spiritual Multiplication in the Real World* (Ch. 8) and answer the

WEEK SEVEN

Chapter 8: Learning to Fly

KEY VERSE

Ephesians 4:11-12
And he gave the apostles, the prophets, the evangelists, the shepherds and teachers, to equip the saints for the work of ministry, for building up the body of Christ,

WORD

Disciple-making and equipping observations	Observations about God

1 Timothy 1

WORSHIP

Praise God for what you saw about him in the Word today.

Today I thank God for...

I will worship God by obeying in the following ways this week:

Today I will trust God for...

WORD

Disciple-making and equipping observations	Observations about God

1 Timothy 2

WORSHIP

Praise God for what you saw about him in the Word today.

Today I thank God for...

I will worship God by obeying in the following ways this week:

Today I will trust God for...

WORD

Disciple-making and equipping observations	Observations about God

1 Timothy 3

WORSHIP

Praise God for what you saw about him in the Word today.

Today I thank God for...

I will worship God by obeying in the following ways this week:

Today I will trust God for...

WORD

Disciple-making and equipping observations	Observations about God

1 Timothy 4

WORSHIP

Praise God for what you saw about him in the Word today.

Today I thank God for...

I will worship God by obeying in the following ways this week:

Today I will trust God for...

WORD

Disciple-making and equipping observations	Observations about God

1 Timothy 5

WORSHIP

Praise God for what you saw about him in the Word today.

Today I thank God for...

I will worship God by obeying in the following ways this week:

Today I will trust God for...

WORD

Disciple-making and equipping observations	Observations about God

1 Timothy 6

WORSHIP

Praise God for what you saw about him in the Word today.

Today I thank God for...

I will worship God by obeying in the following ways this week:

Today I will trust God for...

SUMMARY AND REFLECTION DAY

After looking over this week's quiet times, summarize what God has been teaching you.

What specific action will you take to apply what you have learned?

Did you really meet with Jesus this week, or did you just go through the motions?

WORSHIP

Praise God for what you saw about him in the Word this week.

Today I thank God for...

I will worship God by obeying in the following ways this week:

Today I will trust God for...

▷ Write out this week's Key Verse below:

SPIRITUAL MULTIPLICATION IN THE REAL WORLD (Chapter 8)

1. What is the best example of equipping you have ever seen?

2. What areas of your life are not good models for others?

3. Summarize what you believe were the author's major points regarding selection.

4. Do you agree or disagree with the author's emphasis on character development in the equipping stage of ministry? Why?

5. What is still unclear to you about the equipping phase of ministry?

6. What specific application steps do you believe you need to take in light of what you read in this chapter?

7. With whom will you share what you learned in this chapter?

WELCOME || 15 MINUTES

What have you found to be most helpful in spending quality time alone fellowshipping with God?

WITNESS || 10 MINUTES

What did you see God do this week?

WORSHIP || 10 MINUTES

Thank God together in prayer for what he did last week.

As a group, write down a list of as many of God's attributes as you can.

WORKS || 25 MINUTES

FISHING CHART
Update your FISHing chart with any new people you met this week or steps you took in the FISHing process.

BIG BLUE
Add your team's new friends to Big Blue. Put the list in the middle of the group and pray over your friends.

TOOLS
Pair up and practice The Bridge with another teammate, giving each other feedback.

ACTIVITY
Turn to the Game Plan on the next page and fill in your goals for this week.

WORLD || 10 MINUTES

KNOW GOD'S WORLD: Unreligious

There are 121 million people in 15 Unreligious people groups.[1]

They are mostly atheistic, with some remnants of ancestor worship or Buddhist beliefs.

Many have Communist governments that tell people there is no God.

The majority lives in the country of China.

SHARE HELPFUL RESOURCES
Report on this week's resource: Perspectives on the World Christian Movement (perspectives.org)

Assign next week's resource: Launch Global (launchglobal.org)

PRAY FOR THE NATIONS

WORD || 20 MINUTES

Share Ephesians 4:11-12 with a partner.

Discuss the major learning points and application steps from your Daily Quiet Times (Day 7).

Discuss your answers to the Learning Questions for *Spiritual Multiplication in the Real World* (Ch. 8).

Close with prayer.

GAME PLAN FOR NEXT WEEK

3 HOURS *with Jesus*

Daily Quiet Times
Memorize Key Verse: Matthew 9:37-38

2 HOURS *with lost people*

Share The Bridge
I will share The Bridge with _____ people this week

My ministry partner this week will be _____

1 HOUR *with each other in prayer*

This week I will pray with _____

LEARNING ASSIGNMENT

Read *Spiritual Multiplication in the Real World* (Ch. 9) and answer the Learning Questions

WEEK EIGHT

Chapter 9: The Lost Aspect of Disciple-Making

KEY VERSE

Matthew 9:37-38
Then he said to his disciples, "The harvest is plentiful, but the laborers are few; therefore pray earnestly to the Lord of the harvest to send out laborers into his harvest."

WORD

Observations about God's heart for the nations	General observations about God's character
Psalm 96	

WORSHIP

Praise God for what you saw about him in the Word today.

Today I thank God for...

I will worship God by obeying in the following ways this week:

Today I will trust God for...

WORD

Observations about God's heart for the nations	General observations about God's character

Matthew 9:35-38

WORSHIP

Praise God for what you saw about him in the Word today.

Today I thank God for...

I will worship God by obeying in the following ways this week:

Today I will trust God for...

WORD

Observations about God's heart for the nations	General observations about God's character

Romans 10:5-17

WORSHIP

Praise God for what you saw about him in the Word today.

Today I thank God for...

I will worship God by obeying in the following ways this week:

Today I will trust God for...

WORD

Observations about God's heart for the nations	General observations about God's character

Romans 15

WORSHIP

Praise God for what you saw about him in the Word today.

Today I thank God for...

I will worship God by obeying in the following ways this week:

Today I will trust God for...

WORD

Observations about God's heart for the nations	General observations about God's character

Revelation 5

WORSHIP

Praise God for what you saw about him in the Word today.

Today I thank God for...

I will worship God by obeying in the following ways this week:

Today I will trust God for...

WORD

Observations about God's heart for the nations	Observations about the different ways God may give guidance for missions

2 Timothy 4:9-12

Titus 1:5

Acts 16:1-10

WORSHIP

Praise God for what you saw about him in the Word today.

Today I thank God for...

I will worship God by obeying in the following ways this week:

Today I will trust God for...

SUMMARY AND REFLECTION DAY

After looking over this week's quiet times, summarize what God has been teaching you.

What specific action will you take to apply what you have learned?

Did you really meet with Jesus this week, or did you just go through the motions?

WORSHIP

Praise God for what you saw about him in the Word this week.

Today I thank God for...

I will worship God by obeying in the following ways this week:

Today I will trust God for...

▷ Write out this week's Key Verse below:

SPIRITUAL MULTIPLICATION IN THE REAL WORLD (Chapter 9)

1. What do you think has caused such a great imbalance of laborers in the world today?

2. Why do you think most disciple-makers and church leaders are not more actively mobilizing their people to the unreached?

3. What new things did you learn from this chapter?

4. Is there anything in your life that is keeping you from successfully mobilizing laborers?

5. What action step will you take this week to apply what you learned about exporting?

WELCOME || 15 MINUTES

Were you more of an obedient or disobedient child growing up?

Why do you think you were the way you were?

WITNESS || 10 MINUTES

What did you see God do this week?

WORSHIP || 10 MINUTES

Thank God together in prayer for what he did last week.

Use an iPod, guitar, etc. and sing a few songs together.

WORKS || 25 MINUTES

FISHING CHART
Update your FISHing chart with any new people you met this week or steps you took in the FISHing process.

BIG BLUE
Add your team's new friends to Big Blue. Put the list in the middle of the group and pray over your friends.

TOOLS
The leader should introduce "God's Heart for the Nations" (p. 127) and then demonstrate how to share it.

Pair up and practice "God's Heart for the Nations" with another teammate, giving each other feedback.

ACTIVITY

WORLD || 10 MINUTES

KNOW GOD'S WORLD: Muslim

There are 1.3 billion people in 1,344 Muslim people groups.[1]

They believe in one God, named Allah, and that Mohammad was his final prophet.

They believe if the good deeds done in life outweigh the bad deeds, Muslims go to Paradise when they die.

They respect Jesus as a good prophet but do not believe he is God.

SHARE HELPFUL RESOURCES
Report on this week's resource: Launch Global (launchglobal.org)

Assign next week's resource: Joshua Project (joshuaproject.net)

PRAY FOR THE NATIONS

WORD || 20 MINUTES

Share Matthew 9:37-38 with a partner.

Discuss the major learning points and application steps from your Daily Quiet Times (Day 7).

Discuss your answers to the Learning Questions for *Spiritual Multiplication in the Real World* (Ch. 9).

Close with prayer.

GAME PLAN FOR NEXT WEEK

3 HOURS *with Jesus*

Daily Quiet Times
Memorize Key Verse: 2 Corinthians 3:5-6

2 HOURS *with lost people*

Share God's Heart for the Nations
I will share God's Heart for the Nations with _____ people this week

My ministry partner this week will be _____

1 HOUR *with each other in prayer*

This week I will pray with _____

LEARNING ASSIGNMENT

Read *Spiritual Multiplication in the Real World* (Ch. 10) and answer the Learning Questions

WEEK NINE

Chapter 10: You Can!

KEY VERSE

2 Corinthians 3:5-6
Not that we are sufficient in ourselves to claim anything as coming from us, but our sufficiency is from God, who has made us sufficient to be ministers of a new covenant, not of the letter but of the Spirit. For the letter kills, but the Spirit gives life.

WORD: 1 Timothy 1:18, 4:11-16; 2 Timothy 1:6-7

In what ways was Paul empowering Timothy with his words in 1 Timothy 4:11-16?

To whom should you speak encouraging and empowering truth today?

WORSHIP

Praise God for what you saw about him in the Word today.

Today I thank God for...

I will worship God by obeying in the following ways this week:

Today I will trust God for...

▷ Learn this week's Key Verse.

WORD: Matthew 10:19-20, Acts 1:8

How did Jesus empower his disciples in these verses?

To whom should you speak encouraging and empowering truth today?

WORSHIP

Praise God for what you saw about him in the Word today.

Today I thank God for...

I will worship God by obeying in the following ways this week:

Today I will trust God for...

▷ Review this week's Key Verse.

WORD: Matthew 17:19-21, 21:21

How was Jesus empowering his disciples in these verses?

To whom should you speak encouraging and empowering truth today?

WORSHIP

Praise God for what you saw about him in the Word today.

Today I thank God for...

I will worship God by obeying in the following ways this week:

Today I will trust God for...

▷ Review this week's Key Verse.

WORD: Luke 10:19, Matthew 28:20

What can you learn about empowering from what Jesus said in these verses?

How will you apply these truths to your life and ministry?

WORSHIP

Praise God for what you saw about him in the Word today.

Today I thank God for...

I will worship God by obeying in the following ways this week:

Today I will trust God for...

▷ Review this week's Key Verse.

WORD: 2 Corinthians 3:5-6

In light of these verses, how should you think about your ability to minister to others?

How will you act upon this truth?

WORSHIP

Praise God for what you saw about him in the Word today.

Today I thank God for...

I will worship God by obeying in the following ways this week:

Today I will trust God for...

▷ Review this week's Key Verse.

WORD: Philippians 4:13, 2 Corinthians 12:9-10

How should these verses influence your thinking about what you attempt in ministry?

How will you act upon these truths?

WORSHIP

Praise God for what you saw about him in the Word today.

Today I thank God for...

I will worship God by obeying in the following ways this week:

Today I will trust God for...

SUMMARY AND REFLECTION DAY

After looking over this week's quiet times, summarize what God has been teaching you.

What specific action will you take to apply what you have learned?

Did you really meet with Jesus this week, or did you just go through the motions?

WORSHIP

Praise God for what you saw about him in the Word this week.

Today I thank God for...

I will worship God by obeying in the following ways this week:

Today I will trust God for...

▷ Write out this week's Key Verse below:

SPIRITUAL MULTIPLICATION IN THE REAL WORLD (Chapter 10)

1. Many believers feel ill-equipped to disciple others because they think discipling others is something only a highly knowledgeable and wise person can do. The author presents a different view than this. Explain what you believe the author's view is and your reaction to it.

2. Review the lies that Satan tells people mentioned in Chapter 10. What are the lies you find yourself believing most frequently?

3. If you knew for sure that God's power was upon you and that anything you attempted for him would succeed, what do you believe he would want you to attempt?

WELCOME || 15 MINUTES

Who do you know who is most committed to fulfilling the Great Commission, and what is it that you see in his or her life that makes you select this person?

WITNESS || 10 MINUTES

What did you see God do this week?

WORSHIP || 10 MINUTES

Thank God together in prayer for what he did last week.

Take turns reading a few verses of Psalm 145, stopping to praise God for who he is and what he does.

WORKS || 25 MINUTES

FISHING CHART

Update your FISHing chart with any new people you met this week or steps you took in the FISHing process.

BIG BLUE

Add your team's new friends to Big Blue. Put the list in the middle of the group and pray over your friends.

TOOLS

The leader should introduce "Sharing the Vision of Multiplication" (p. 125) and then demonstrate how to share it.

Pair up and practice "Sharing the Vision of Multiplication" with another teammate, giving each other feedback.

ACTIVITY

WORLD || 10 MINUTES

KNOW GOD'S WORLD: Buddhists

There are 275 million people in 227 Buddhist people groups.[1]

They believe that suffering is caused by desire.

To end suffering, they must rid themselves of desire through meditation and multiple reincarnations.

The ultimate goal is to reach Nirvana, where suffering ends and the self ceases to exist.

SHARE HELPFUL RESOURCES

Report on this week's resource: Joshua Project (joshuaproject.net)

Assign next week's resource: The Traveling Team (thetravelingteam.org)

PRAY FOR THE NATIONS

WORD || 20 MINUTES

Share 2 Corinthians 3:5-6 with a partner.

Discuss the major learning points and application steps from your Daily Quiet Times (Day 7).

Discuss your answers to the Learning Questions for *Spiritual Multiplication in the Real World* (Ch. 10).

Close with prayer.

GAME PLAN FOR NEXT WEEK

3 HOURS *with Jesus*

Daily Quiet Times
Memorize Key Verse: Galatians 6:9

2 HOURS *with lost people*

This week, the evangelistic activity I will do is: _____
I will do an evangelistic activity with _____ people this week

Share the Vision for Spiritual Multiplication
I will share the Vision for Spiritual Multiplication with _____ people this week

My ministry partner this week will be _____

1 HOUR *with each other in prayer*

This week I will pray with _____

LEARNING ASSIGNMENT

Read *Spiritual Multiplication in the Real World* (Ch. 11) and answer the

WEEK TEN

Chapter 11: From Vision to Reality

KEY VERSE

Galatians 6:9
And let us not grow weary of doing good, for in due season we will reap, if we do not give up.

WORD

Requirements for Multiplication	Observations about God

Mark 4

What does this passage teach will be required to see your vision of spiritual multiplication become a reality?

WORSHIP

Praise God for what you saw about him in the Word today.

Today I thank God for...

I will worship God by obeying in the following ways this week:

Today I will trust God for...

WORD

Requirements for Multiplication	Observations about God

John 15

What does this passage teach will be required to see your vision of spiritual multiplication become a reality?

WORSHIP

Praise God for what you saw about him in the Word today.

Today I thank God for...

I will worship God by obeying in the following ways this week:

Today I will trust God for...

WORD: Matthew 6:24, 2 Timothy 2:4, John 12:20-26

What do these passages teach will be required to see your vision of spiritual multiplication become a reality?

What do you need to do to apply what is taught in these verses?

WORSHIP

Praise God for what you saw about him in the Word today.

Today I thank God for...

I will worship God by obeying in the following ways this week:

Today I will trust God for...

WORD: Hebrews 4:14-16

What does this passage teach will be required to see your vision of spiritual multiplication become a reality?

What do you need to do to apply what is taught in these verses?

WORSHIP

Praise God for what you saw about him in the Word today.

Today I thank God for...

I will worship God by obeying in the following ways this week:

Today I will trust God for...

WORD: Revelation 2:1-7

What does this passage teach will be required to see your vision of spiritual multiplication become a reality?

What do you need to do to apply what is taught in these verses?

WORSHIP

Praise God for what you saw about him in the Word today.

Today I thank God for...

I will worship God by obeying in the following ways this week:

Today I will trust God for...

WORD: Galatians 6:9, 1 Corinthians 15:58

What do these passages teach will be required to see your vision of spiritual multiplication become a reality?

What do you need to do to apply what is taught in these verses?

WORSHIP

Praise God for what you saw about him in the Word today.

Today I thank God for...

I will worship God by obeying in the following ways this week:

Today I will trust God for...

SUMMARY AND REFLECTION DAY

After looking over this week's quiet times, summarize what God has been teaching you.

What specific action will you take to apply what you have learned?

Did you really meet with Jesus this week, or did you just go through the motions?

WORSHIP

Praise God for what you saw about him in the Word this week.

Today I thank God for...

I will worship God by obeying in the following ways this week:

Today I will trust God for...

▷ Write out this week's Key Verse below:

SPIRITUAL MULTIPLICATION IN THE REAL WORLD (Chapter 11)

1. After reading about the direct relationship between one's time alone with God and one's fruitfulness in ministry, do you need to make any changes in your devotional practices? If so, what are they?

2. What "other visions" or "cares of the world" do you need to deal with if you are going to multiply your life?

3. Which of the "First Steps" do you need to take?

4. What are some of the things in your plan that you are trusting God to do through your life?

5. Whom are you going to ask to team up with you in the mission of disciple-making?

6. If you gave up on disciple-making one day in the future, what do you think would be the reason?

7. The author described our mission in this way, "As part of a disciple-making team, go and multiply disciple-making teams in all nations." Do you think explaining our mission in this way is helpful? Why or why not?

WELCOME || 15 MINUTES

Share how this group has helped you over the last nine weeks.

WITNESS || 10 MINUTES

What did you see God do this week?

WORSHIP || 10 MINUTES

Thank God together in prayer for what he did last week.

Use an iPod, guitar, etc. and sing a few songs together.

WORKS || 25 MINUTES

FISHING CHART
Update your FISHing chart with any new people you met this week or steps you took in the FISHing process.

BIG BLUE
Add your team's new friends to Big Blue. Spend an extended time praying for all of your friends on this list.

ACTIVITY
Discuss and fill out "My Disciple-Making Plan" on p. 129.

Discuss the future of your team.

WORLD || 10 MINUTES

KNOW GOD'S WORLD: Internationals

There are over 680,000 international students who study and live in the United States every year.[5]

Sixty percent of international students come from the 10/40 Window.

Forty percent of the world's 220 Heads of State once studied in the US.

Eighty percent of these students will return to their countries having never been invited to an American home.[4]

SHARE HELPFUL RESOURCES
Report on this week's resource: The Traveling Team (thetravelingteam.org)

PRAY FOR THE NATIONS

WORD || 20 MINUTES

Share Galatians 6:9 with a partner.

Discuss the major learning points and application steps from your Daily Quiet Times (Day 7).

Discuss your answers to the Learning Questions for *Spiritual Multiplication in the Real World* (Ch. 11).

Close with prayer.

APPENDIX

FISHING CHART

MY STORY: CREATING INTEREST TESTIMONY

FIND: QUESTIONS

GLOSSARY

BRIDGE ILLUSTRATION

SHARING THE VISION FOR MULTIPLICATION

GOD'S HEART FOR THE NATIONS

MY DISCIPLE-MAKING PLAN

FISHING CHART

#	FIND				INTEREST				SHARE				HELP	
Name	Interests	Felt Needs	Attitude Toward Jesus	Testimony	Answered Prayer Stories	Community	Prayer for their needs	Jesus Story	Discovery Bible Study	Gospel Presentation	Something to Read	Ask for a Decision	Deal with Barriers

FISHING CHART

# Name	FIND			INTEREST				SHARE				HELP	
	Interests	Felt Needs	Attitude Toward Jesus	Testimony	Answered Prayer Stories	Community	Prayer for their needs	Jesus Story	Discovery Bible Study	Gospel Presentation	Something to Read	Ask for a Decision	Deal with Barriers

Interest Creating Needs

I first sensed my need for Jesus when...
Hard to pin point, but definetly since I was a small child houshold

What made me most interested in Jesus was...
That he loved the the rejected people. And the rejected loved him

I finally decided to trust Jesus and follow him when I realized that...
I needed to ~~have~~ love him back ~~+ start the~~ take my first ~~by disciple~~ step of baptism. Then accepting the bible as truth from god.

Since I entered into a relationship with Jesus, I have changed

From: letting culture tell me what's right & wrong

To: Finding joy in doing what god mandates as right

From: Valuing my lifestyle more than ~~my relationship~~ trying to become closer to christ

To: Valuing christ more than my lifestyle.

Jesus helps me in my daily life by...
Giving me a hope. He has been with me.

I have seen God answer my prayers in some pretty cool ways, like the time...

When meeting new people, the easiest way to begin getting to know [them is by asking] questions. It is usually best to start by asking biographical question[s and then move on to] more personal questions about their interests and needs. Take a min[ute to look] over the following example questions. Then take turns practicing asking questions and moving the conversation from biographical to interests to needs.

1. **Biographical questions:**

    Where are you from?

    Where do you live now?

    What do you do?

    Tell me about your family.

2. **Interests questions:** (Hopefully, these questions will help you find some ways you can spend time together in the future.)

    Do you have any hobbies or favorite sports?

    What is your favorite thing to do in your free time?

3. **Needs questions:**

    I try to pray for the needs of people I meet. Is there anything specific I can pray for you?

THE LEGEND OF BIG BLUE

In 2007, a dedicated group of believers in Iowa began to meet as a missional community. A cornerstone of their weekly meetings was a time of prayer for the lost. Names of lost friends were written on a leftover piece of blue flooring material, which was then laid in the middle of the room to be prayed over. Each week, as members recalled people they had met, new names were added to the list. A time of intense prayer would follow as disciples got on their knees to pray over "Big Blue." As these groups multiplied and spread to other states, so did the inclusion of Big Blue. Get a blue piece of fabric or poster board and join the movement!

MATTHEW PARTY

A Matthew Party is a get-together planned for people who need to meet Jesus. We get the name from Matthew, the tax collector, who held a reception in his home for people to come meet Jesus. One of the goals of this event is to allow our lost friends to experience the difference Christ makes in a community of believers. It is important that we aren't outnumbered, as seeing Christ-centered community in action is the goal behind this gathering. We want them to see the love we have for one another. A Matthew Party can be a dinner, a game night, bowling, ice skating, some sort of cultural activity, etc. The important thing is allowing our lost friends to spend time with a group of believers.

LUKE 5:29-32 (ESV)

And Levi [Matthew] made him [Jesus] a great feast in his house, and there was a large company of tax collectors and others reclining at table with them. And the Pharisees and their scribes grumbled at his disciples, saying, "Why do you eat and drink with tax collectors and sinners?"

And Jesus answered them, "Those who are well have no need of a physician, but those who are sick. I have not come to call the righteous but sinners to repentance."

JOHN 13:35

By this all people will know that you are my disciples, if you have love for one another.

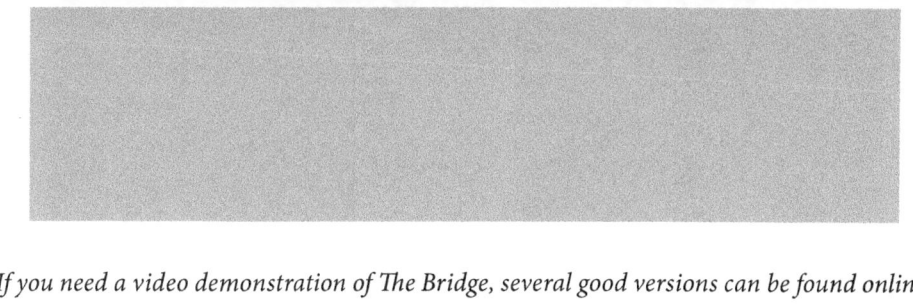

If you need a video demonstration of The Bridge, several good versions can be found online.

WHAT JESUS DID

The Twelve — Jesus

Peter
James
John

Inner _Circle_

WHAT JESUS COMMANDED

"Therefore go and _make_ _disciples_ of _nations_, baptizing them in the name of the Father and of the Son and of the Holy Spirit."

Matthew 28:19

WHAT JESUS PROMISED

"Others, like seed sown on good soil, hear the word, accept it, and produce a crop—some _30_, some _60_, some _100_ times what was sown."

Mark 4:20

WHAT PAUL DID

"And what you have heard from me in the presence of many witnesses entrust to faithful men who will be able to teach others also."

2 Timothy 2:2

Paul → Silas, Titus
Timothy → _faithful_, _faithful men_
faithful men → _others_, _others_, _others_, _others_

YOUR POTENTIAL IMPACT

If you only discipled two people per year and taught them to multiply each year, you could multiply over _3 Billion_ disciples in just twenty years.

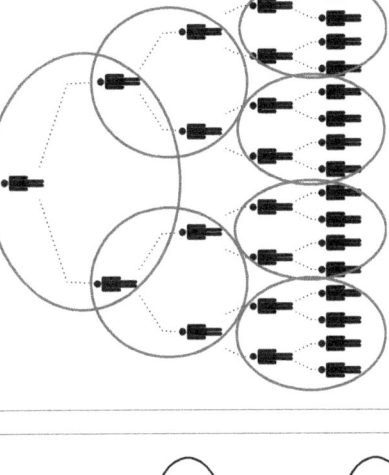

- ☐ Draw circles around groups of disciples and discuss the importance of multiplying not only disciples, but disciple-making teams.

WHAT ACTION WILL YOU TAKE?

- ☐ I will seek out someone to disciple me.
- ☐ I will seek out people to disciple.

WHAT JESUS DID

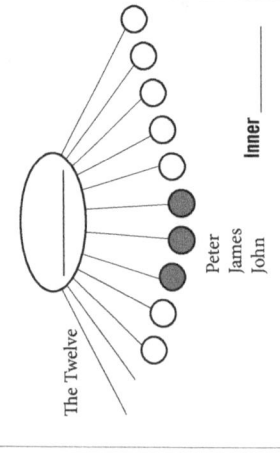

The Twelve

Peter
James
John

Inner _____

WHAT JESUS COMMANDED

"Therefore go and _____ of the name of the Father and of the Son and of the Holy Spirit."

Matthew 28:19

WHAT JESUS PROMISED

"Others, like seed sown on good soil, hear the word, accept it, and produce a crop—some _____, some _____, some _____ times what was sown."

Mark 4:20

WHAT PAUL DID

"And what you have heard from me in the presence of many witnesses entrust to faithful men who will be able to teach others also."

2 Timothy 2:2

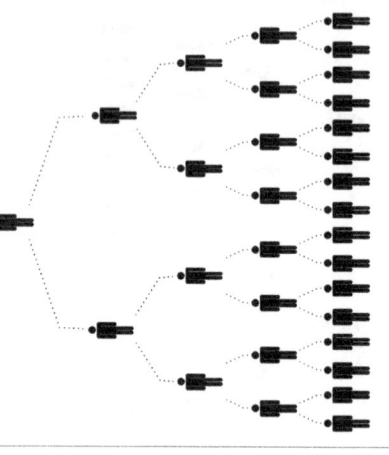

YOUR POTENTIAL IMPACT

If you only discipled two people per year and taught them to multiply each year, you could multiply over 3 _____ disciples in just twenty years.

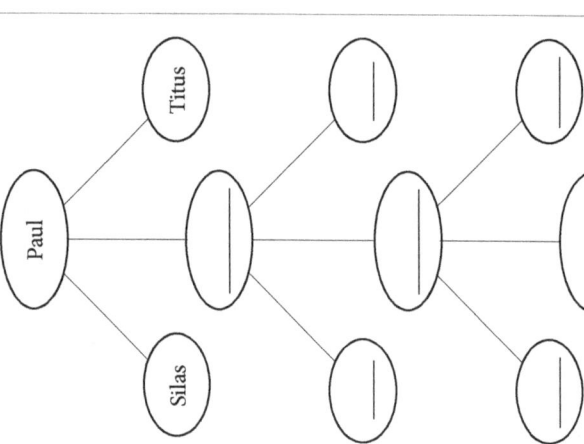

☐ Draw circles around groups of disciples and discuss the importance of multiplying not only disciples, but disciple-making teams.

WHAT ACTION WILL YOU TAKE?

☐ I will seek out someone to disciple me.
☐ I will seek out people to disciple.

THE GRAND NARRATIVE

1. Commission to multiply God's image bearers in all the earth: **Genesis 1:28**
2. Image marred: **Genesis 3:15**
3. People Groups Formed: **Genesis 11:8**
4. God's plan to bless all nations through Abraham's Children: **Genesis 12:2-3**
5. Example of an Old Testament imperative to preach to the nations: **1 Chronicles 16:24**
6. All believers are children of Abraham and have the same blessings and responsibilities: **Galatians 3:7-9**
7. The gospel of the kingdom and the demonstration of its power went to the rst: **Matthew 10:6-8**
8. The blessing is supposed to spread to all nations: **Acts 1:8**
9. Jesus has commanded all of his followers to spread his kingdom to the nations (ethne): **Matthew 28:18-20**
10. We should make the unreached our ambition: **Romans 15:20**
11. Jesus ransomed all nations: **Revelation 5:9**

All nations will be in heaven: **Revelation 7:9**

---

2 THE GREAT IMBALANCE

- **60% Reached**
- _40_ **% Unreached**

The average American spends **$20 per week** on coffee.

The average American Christian gives ___1.5 cents___ to the unreached each week.

---

3 YOUR PART

WHAT DO YOU THINK IS YOUR MOST STRATEGIC ROLE?

1. Go
2. Give
3. Pray
4. _Welcome_
5. _Mobilize_
6. _Other:_

WHAT DO YOU THINK IS YOUR MOST STRATEGIC LOCATION?

Sending	Reached
Unengaged	_Unreached_

WHAT DO YOU THINK IS YOUR MOST STRATEGIC NEXT STEP?

THE GRAND NARRATIVE

1. Commission to multiply God's image bearers in all the earth: **Genesis 1:28**
2. Image marred: **Genesis 3:15**
3. People Groups Formed: **Genesis 11:8**
4. God's plan to bless all nations through Abraham's Children: **Genesis 12:2-3**
5. Example of an Old Testament imperative to preach to the nations: **1 Chronicles 16:24**
6. All believers are children of Abraham and have the same blessings and responsibilities: **Galatians 3:7-9**
7. The gospel of the kingdom and the demonstration of its power went to the first: **Matthew 10:6-8**
8. The blessing is supposed to spread to all nations: **Acts 1:8**
9. Jesus has commanded all of his followers to spread his kingdom to the nations (ethne): **Matthew 28:18-20**
10. We should make the unreached our ambition: **Romans 15:20**
11. Jesus ransomed all nations: **Revelation 5:9**

All nations will be in heaven: **Revelation 7:9**

2 THE GREAT IMBALANCE

60% Reached

____% Unreached

The average American spends **$20 per week** on coffee.

The average American Christian gives _____ to the unreached each week.

3 YOUR PART

WHAT DO YOU THINK IS YOUR MOST STRATEGIC ROLE?

1. Go
2. Give
3. Pray
4. _____
5. _____
6. _____

WHAT DO YOU THINK IS YOUR MOST STRATEGIC LOCATION?

Sending	**Reached**
_____	_____

WHAT DO YOU THINK IS YOUR MOST STRATEGIC NEXT STEP?

VISION: I would like to see the following vision become a reality:

TRUSTING GOD: I am trusting God to do the following:

>Before I die:

>In the next three years:

>In the next twelve months:

>In the next three months:

>I am claiming the following promises from God's Word:

SHARING THE VISION: I will ask the following people to join me in the vision and to speak into it:

PIN IT UP: I will put a visual reminder in the following places:

FOUNDATIONS:
MISSIONAL COMMUNITY GUIDEBOOK

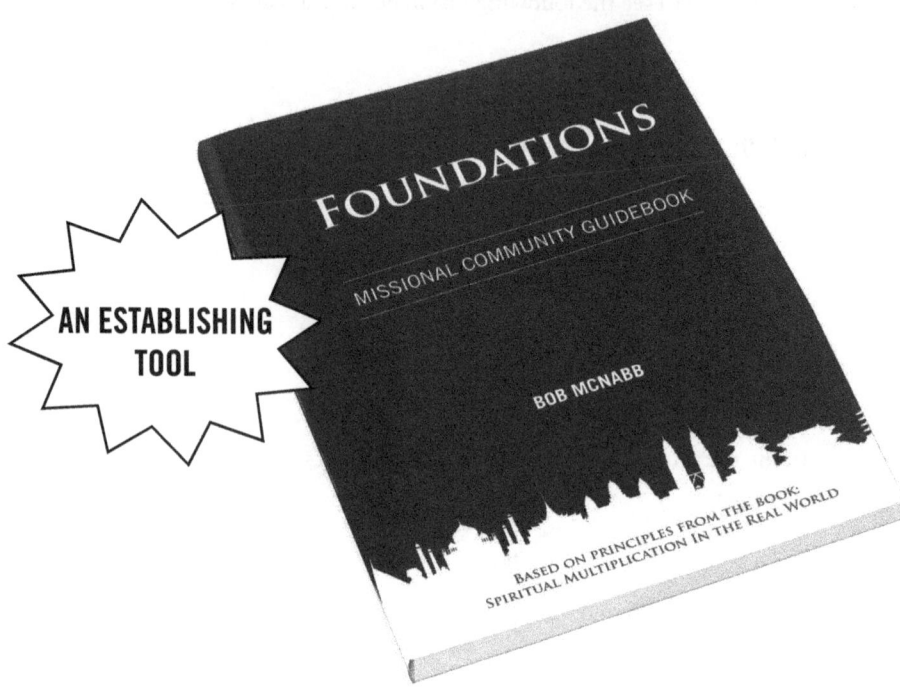

This resource is designed to lead new believers into missional community and outreach while establishing them in the foundations of the faith. Together, disciples learn how to grow spiritually and bear fruit as obedient followers of Christ. Foundations is a proven tool to practically build up your disciples in the basics of a Christ-centered life while they reach out to others as a community. It will solidify their faith through the study of the following lessons:

Week 1: My Story
Week 2: The Gospel
Week 3: Assurance of Salvation
Week 4: Following Christ as Lord
Week 5: Living in Grace
Week 6: Purpose in Life

Week 7: Quiet Time
Week 8: The Word
Week 9: Prayer
Week 10: Life in the Spirit
Week 11: Perseverance in Suffering

1. *The Task Remaining* by Ralph D. Winter and Bruce A. Koch, *Perspectives on the World Christian Movement, Reader.* 4th ed. William Carey Library, 2009, p.531-546. *www.missionbooks.org*

2. Joshua Project, *www.joshuaproject.org*

3. *The Coming Revolution: Because Status Quo Missions Won't Finish the Job* by Mark R. Baxter, Tate Publishing, 2007, p.12.

4. The Traveling Team, *www.thetravelingteam.org*

5. Statistics from The Institute of International Education, Inc. *www.iie.org*